Year 4

Non-Fiction Writing

by Sue Garnett

Introduction

Photocopiable Non-Fiction Writing for Year 4 is designed as an aid to the busy classroom teacher planning non-fiction writing activities for the Literacy Strategy.

The author has written a selection of non-fiction example texts covering the different genres required by the Literacy Strategy. These are accompanied by Writing Frames to help children to carefully plan and carry out their own piece of writing after study of each example.

For those children who struggle to think up ideas, or who have special needs, there are writing support sheets for each activity.

The main points to remember about each different type of non-fiction writing are summarised at the beginning of each section of the book. These may be enlarged and turned into wall posters to use as a constant reminder of the points made.

Topical Resources, P.O. Box 329, Broughton, Preston, Lancashire. PR3 5LT

Topical Resources publishes a range of Educational Materials for use in Primary Schools and Pre-School Nurseries and Playgroups.

For the latest catalogue:
Tel 01772 863158
Fax 01772 866153
e.mail:sales@topical-resources.co.uk
Visit our Website at:
www.topical-resources.co.uk

Copyright © 2002 Sue Garnett
Illustrated by John Hutchinson & Paul Sealey

Typeset by Paul Sealey Illustration & Design,
3 Wentworth Drive, Thornton, Lancashire.

Printed in Great Britain for 'Topical Resources', Publishers of Educational Materials, P.O. Box 329, Broughton, Preston, Lancashire PR3 5LT by T.Snape & Company Limited, Boltons Court, Preston Lancashire.

First Published April 2002
ISBN 1 872977 67 7

Notes for Teachers

Non Fiction for Year 4 is designed to develop children's writing skills in non fiction. The photocopiable book contains different types of non fiction writing models and worksheets.

Aims
The book aims to improve children's writing skills by providing them with a model and then another similar idea for them to write about using a framework and following the features of that writing.

How does it work?
The book is divided into different types of non fiction writing. Within each type of writing there are several models each consisting of three pages.

First Page
- This is a model of the type of writing.
- The teacher reads the model with the children.
- The teacher discusses the model looking closely at the features of it, the grammar and vocabulary used and the layout.

Second Page
- This is a work page for children who need more support, ideas and guidance. The teacher will discuss the work sheet with the children in detail and help them complete it.
- The work sheet has information about the features of that type of writing. The teacher should read it through with the children.
- The worksheet has information about how to plan the ideas and set out the piece of writing. The teacher should explain how to use it.
- This worksheet has a word bank. It gives the children ideas and correct spellings to help them with their work.
- After the children have filled it in, they will use it to help them write their final piece of work which may be in an exercise book or on a piece of paper.

Third Page
- This is a work page which most of the children in the class will use to jot down their ideas before writing a final piece of work on separate paper. The teacher will discuss the work sheet before the children use it.
- The work sheet has information about the features of that type of writing. The teacher should read it through with the children.
- The work sheet has information about how to plan the ideas and set out the piece of writing. The teacher should explain how to use it.
- After the children have filled it in, they will use it to help them write their final piece of work which may be in an exercise book or on a piece of paper.

Contents

Instructions

- Tell you how to make or do something

- Have a list of things you may need e.g. card, pens, paint brush

- Have a numbered list

- Are written in an order that cannot be changed around.

Example 1

Find the Pirate Treasure

What you will need

- Map
- Key
- Compass
- Spade

Instructions

1 Get off the boat at the landing stage on Pearl Beach.

2 Walk 100 paces North into the forest.

3 Cross the river.

4 Take the path East to the rock face.

5 Climb the rock face.

6 Turn North and take the path to the cave.

7 Enter the cave.

8 Walk 25 paces North.

9 Dig a hole 1metre deep.

10 Find treasure chest and open with the key to see what is inside.

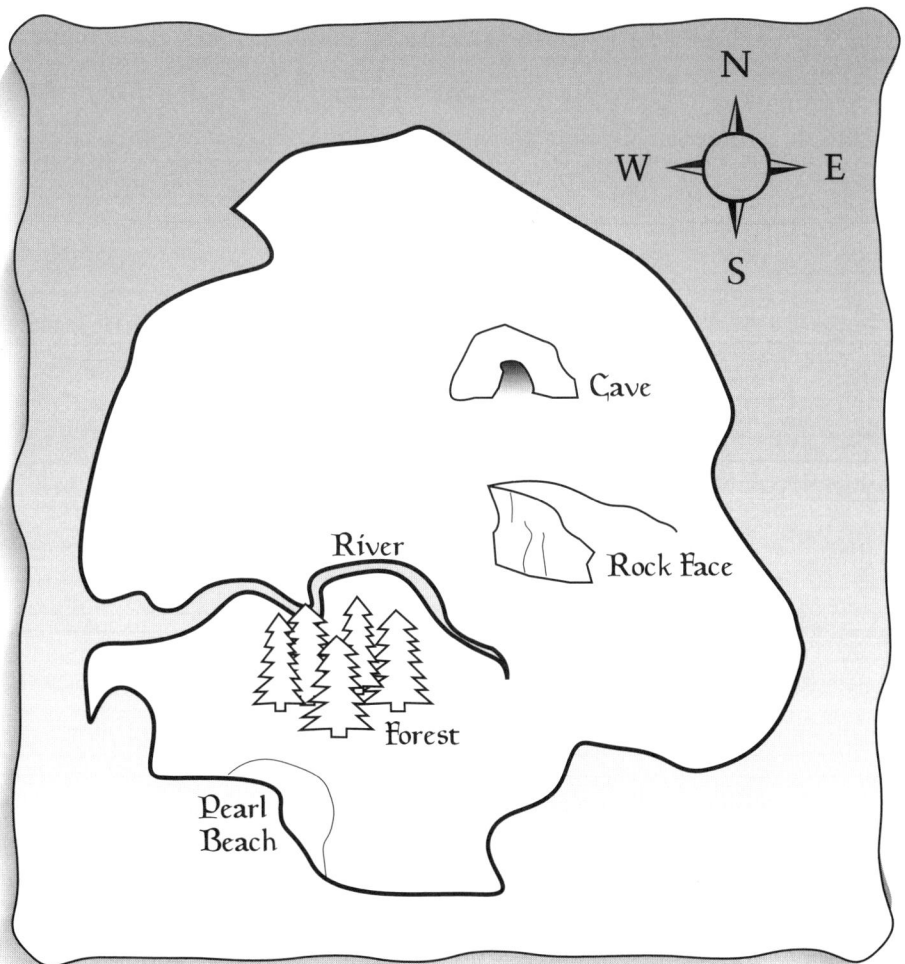

How to Write Instructions

Name: _____ **Date:** _____

Write your own instructions for finding buried treasure.

Instructions
- Have a numbered list
- May have a list of what you need
- May have a simple map.

Planning Instructions
- Draw a sketch map first
- Put lots of places on the map
- Plan how to get to them

Ideas for a treasure map:

Word Bank

beach

forest

river

pool

mountain

cliffs

cave

hole

treasure

chest

walk

cross

climb

turn

enter

dig

find

Ideas for the instructions:

Title: _____

1

2

3

4

5

How to Write
Instructions

Name:_____ **Date:** _____

Write your own instructions for finding buried treasure.

Instructions	Planning Instructions
• Have a numbered list • May have a list of what you need • May have a map or diagram	• Draw a sketch map first • Put lots of places on the map • Plan how to get to them

Ideas for the instructions:

Title:

_____

_____

_____

Ideas for a treasure map:

1

2

3

4

5

6

7

FANCY DRESS COSTUME

Roman Emperor

What you will need:
- White sheet
- Cord
- Green card
- Scissors
- Glue

How to make the toga:
1 Fold the sheet in half.
2 Cut a hole for the head.
3 Put cloth over the child's body.
4 Cut to fit height of child.
5 Tie the cord around the waist.

How to make the laurel head band:
1 Cut out laurel leaves from green card.
2 Cut out a headband about 5cm wide.
3 Stick leaves on to head band.
4 Place on head.

How to Write Instructions

Name: _____ **Date:** _____

Write a set of instructions for making a fancy dress hat.

Instructions	Planning Instructions
• Have a numbered list • May have a list of things you need • May have a simple sketch.	• Draw the fancy dress hat • Make a list of things you need • Write down how to make it.

Sketch of a fancy dress hat:

Title:
_____
_____
_____

Things you need to make it:

Word Bank

fancy

hat

scissors

ruler

glue

card

paper

pencil

pens

cut

tie

stick

fold

put

How to make it:

1

2

3

4

5

How to Write Instructions

Name:_____ **Date:** _____

Write a set of instructions for making a fancy dress hat.

Instructions
• Have a numbered list
• May have a list of things you need
• May have a diagram.

Planning Instructions
• Draw the fancy dress hat
• Make a list of things you need
• Write down how to make it.

Diagram:

Title:
_____

_____

Things you need to make it:

How to make it:

1

2

3

4

5

Example 3

How to Make a
Humpty Dumpty
Decorated Egg

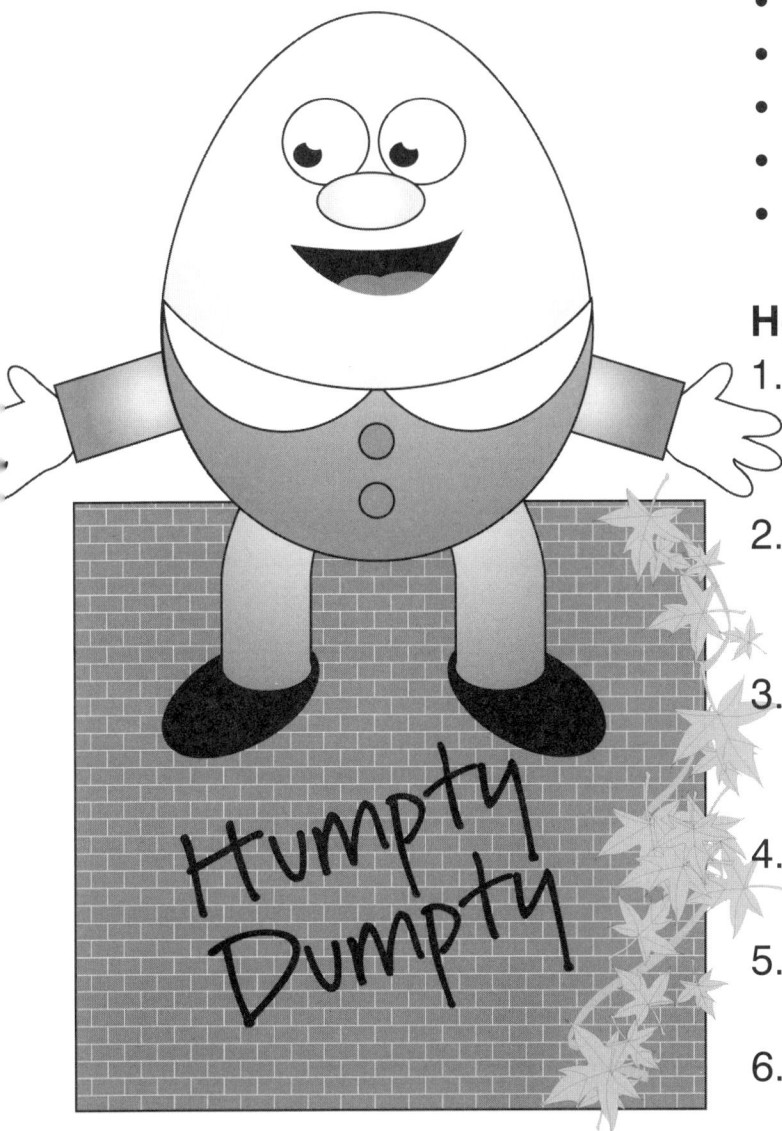

What you will need:

- Hard boiled egg
- Felt tip pens
- Box
- Card
- Paint and paint brush

How to make it:

1. Draw a face on the top half of the egg.

2. Colour bottom half of egg to look like clothes.

3. Cut out card arms and legs and colour with felt tip pens.

4. Stick them to the egg.

5. Paint the box to look like a wall.

6. Glue Humpty Dumpty to the top of the wall.

How to Write Instructions

Name: _____ **Date:** _____

Write your own instructions for a decorated egg.

Instructions
- Have a numbered list
- May have a list of things you need
- May have a simple sketch.

Planning Instructions
- Draw the decorated egg
- Write down what you need to make it
- Write down how to make it.

Sketch of a decorated egg:

Title:
_____
_____
_____

Things you need to make it:

Word Bank

cartoon

character

nursery

rhyme

egg

card

material

glue

pens

paint

brush

draw

cut

stick

paint

decorate

How to make it:

1

2

3

4

5

How to Write Instructions

Writing Frame

Name:_____ **Date:** _____

Write your own instructions for a decorated egg

Instructions
- Have a numbered list
- May have a list of things you need
- May have a diagram.

Planning Instructions
- Draw the decorated egg
- Write down what you need to make it
- Write down how to make it step by step.

Diagram:

Title:
_____
_____

Things you need to make it:

How to make it:

1

2

3

4

5

Non-Chronological Reports

- Have a title

- Have an introduction

- Each paragraph tells us something different

- You can swap the paragraphs around except for the introduction

- Are factual e.g. "The buttercup can grow as high as 30cm."

- May have headings and sub headings e.g. Buttercup, Daisy, Dandelion, Bluebell.

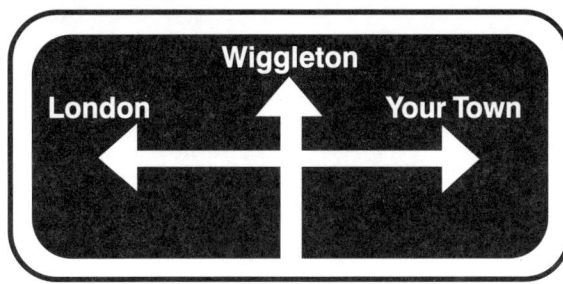

Fun for the Family in Wiggleton

There are lots of things to see and do in Wiggleton.

Wiggleton Castle

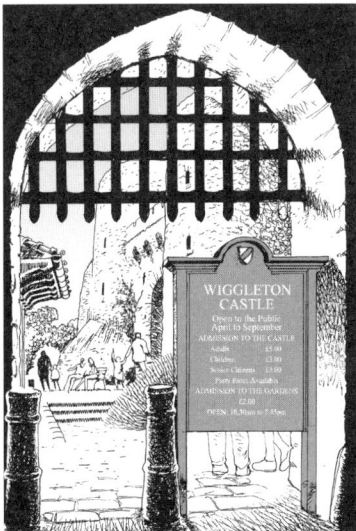

Wiggleton castle is very old. It has a moat and a wooden bridge. There are four towers. There is a dungeon where prisoners were kept.

Wiggleton Park

Wiggleton Park is exciting. There are forest walks and a nature trail. There is a boating lake where you can hire a rowing boat. There is a playground for young children and an adventure playground with a zip wire.

Splash Water Centre

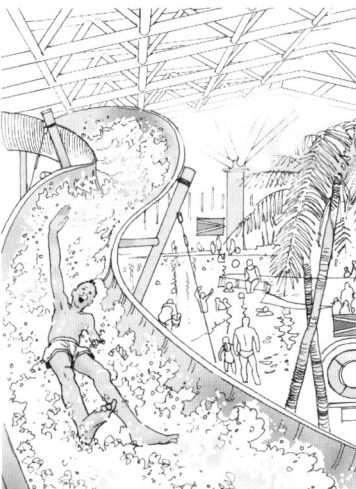

The water centre is in the middle of town. It has a 25 metre pool. There is a fun pool with water shoots and a wave machine. There are inflatable toys to use during the holidays and there is a café.

Wiggleton Museum

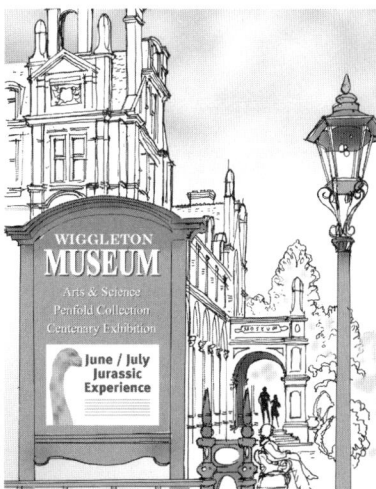

There are lots of things here from long ago like pots, paintings, old bones and fossils. There is a shop where you can buy post cards.

How to Write a Non-Chronological Report

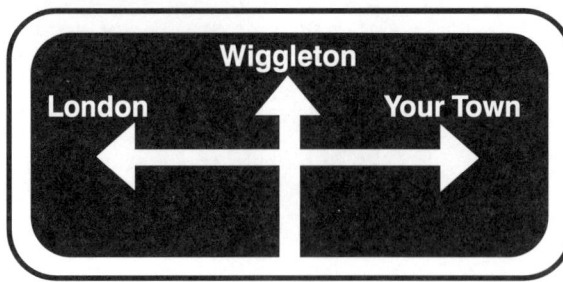

Wiggleton
London ← ↑ → Your Town

Name: _____ **Date:** _____

Write a report about a town to visit. (It could be your town.)

A Non Chronological Report

- Has an introduction
- Has headings
- Is written in paragraphs
- Has lots of facts.

Planning Your Report

- Write an opening sentence
- Think of 3 headings
- Write lots of facts.

Ideas for a report:

Title: _____

First sentence:

Heading:

Ideas:

Heading:

Ideas:

Heading:

Ideas:

Word Bank

castle

swimming

pool

theatre

museum

shops

park

river

places to

visit

enjoy

have fun

old/new

exciting

interesting

shops/cafes

souvenirs

How to Write a Non-Chronological Report

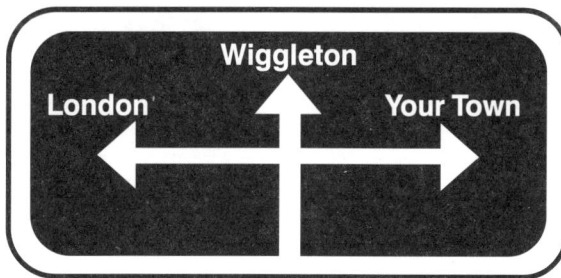

Wiggleton

London ← ↑ → Your Town

Writing Frame

Name:_____ **Date:** _____

Write a report about a town to visit. (It could be your town.)

A Non-Chronological Report
- Has an introduction
- Has headings
- Is written in paragraphs
- Has lots of facts.

Planning Your Report
- Write an opening sentence
- Think of 3 or 4 headings
- Write lots of facts.

Ideas e.g.- castle, swimming pool, theatre, museum, park, shops

Title:
_____

Introduction:

Heading:

Ideas:

Heading:

Ideas:

Heading:

Ideas:

Heading:

Ideas:

Wild Flowers

There are many different types of wild flowers. They are found in different sizes, shapes and colours. They can live in many different places.

Buttercup

The buttercup can be found in meadows and fields It can grow as high as 30cm. It has a golden yellow flower with five petals. It is poisonous to animals.

Daisy

The daisy can be found everywhere. It is the most common wild flower. The flower head is yellow in the middle and has many white petals around it. The petals close up at night and during wet weather.

Dandelion

The dandelion can be found in most places. It has no proper stem. The flower head is long and golden. After the flower has died it looks like a fluffy ball. The seeds float away in the wind.

Bluebell

The bluebell can be found in woods, hedges and shady places. It can grow up to 30cm. The flower is bell shaped. It blooms in April and May.

How to Write a Non-Chronological Report

Name: _____ **Date:** _____

Write a non chronological report about trees.

A Non Chronological Report
- Has an introduction
- Has headings
- Is written in paragraphs
- Has lots of facts.

Planning Your Report
- Write an opening sentence
- Think of 3 headings
- Write lots of facts under each heading.

Ideas for the report:

Title: _____

First sentence:

Heading:

Ideas:

Heading:

Ideas:

Heading:

Ideas:

Word Bank

countryside

towns

fields

parks

gardens

spring

blossom

leaves

autumn

fruit

horse chestnut

conkers

oak

acorns

beech

nuts

fir trees

pine cones

How to Write a Non-Chronological Report

Name:_____ **Date:** _____

Write a non chronological report about trees.

A Non Chronological Report
- Has an introduction
- Has headings
- Is written in paragraphs
- Has lots of facts.

Planning Your Report
- Write an opening sentence
- Think of 4 headings
- Write lots of facts under each heading.

Ideas e.g. trees – horse chestnut, oak, beech, fir, etc.

Title: _____

First sentence:

Heading:

Ideas:

Heading:

Ideas:

Heading:

Ideas:

Heading:

Ideas:

News Reports

- Are about events which interest the public

- Explain points clearly

- Give lots of information

- May have quotes telling what people have said.

Example 1

Education News

4th February 2002   **Issue 18**

CHILDREN IN PRINT
By A. Pencil

Children from schools in Derwent Education Authority have written their own book of poems about their town.

A Liverpool poet, Kerry Taffrey, visited the schools to give the children ideas before they went out to write their poems.

The children, teachers and parents attended the book launch at Bigburn

Rovers Football Ground on Friday 1st February. The children read out their poems and some of the children acted out the history of the town in poetic verse.

Sue Garner the project co-ordinator said, "The children enjoyed writing the poems and they were very happy to receive their own copies of the book."

The Director for Derwent Education Authority, Mr Larry Pevendort said, "We are very proud of the children and schools who took part. This is a wonderful achievement."

22

How to Write a News Report

Writing Support Sheet

Name: _____ **Date:** _____

Write a news report about something exciting that has happened at your school.

News Reports
- Are written in columns
- Have a headline
- Include what someone said
- Have a picture.

Planning a Report
Remember the 4Ws

Who?   When?

Where?   What?

Ideas for a news report:

Headline _____

Who?

When?

Where?

What ?

Include what someone said:

Useful Ideas

What?

play

performance

famous person

theatre group

musician

magician

Word Bank

visited

school

children

teachers

headteacher

enjoyed

excited

How to Write a
News Report

Writing Frame

Name:_____ **Date:** _____

Write a news report about something exciting that has happened at your school.

News Reports
- Are written in columns
- Have a headline
- Have a quote of what someone has said
- Have a picture of the event.

Planning a Report

Remember the 4Ws

Who?　　　When?

Where?　　What?

Ideas e.g. sports event; play; class assembly; important visitor; community event etc.

Headline: _____

Who?

When?

Where?

What ?

Quote:

Kilroy was here

Example 2

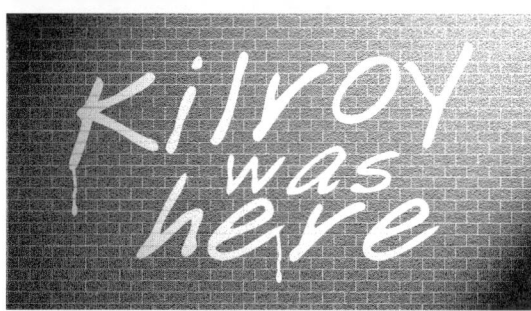

The Evening Star
Wednesday 7th July

Cruelty to Kittens

Report by C.A.T. Lover

Six kittens were found in the River Ribble by local boys on Sunday afternoon.

Harry Moss and Tom Wilson, both aged 8, were riding their bikes down by the river. They stopped to throw stones in the water and saw a black bag in the river, caught on a rock.

"The bag was moving," said Harry. "So I took off my shoes and went to look."
Harry and Tom had a shock when they found a bag full of wet kittens.

"Someone must have put them in the bag to kill them," said Tom. The boys took the kittens to the RSPCA. Luckily there was no harm done and new homes have been found for every one.

25

How to Write a News Report

Kilroy was here

Name: _____ **Date:** _____

Write a news report about something happening in your town which makes you angry or upset.

News Reports
- Are written in columns
- Have a headline
- Write what someone says
- Have a picture of the event.

Planning a Report
Remember the 4Ws

Who?   When?

Where?   What?

Ideas for a news report:

Headline: _____

Who?

When?

Where?

What ?

Include what someone said:

Useful Ideas

What?
cruelty to animals
vandalism
graffiti
burglaries
stolen cars
muggings

Word Bank

horrible
disgusting
mean
cruel
frightening
pointless

How to Write a News Report

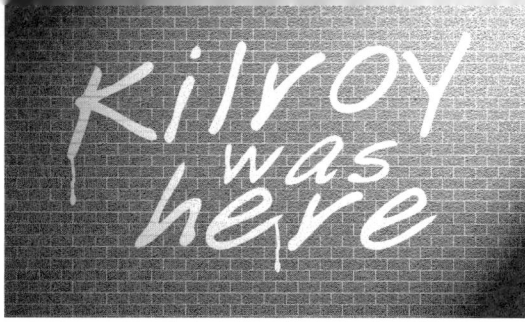

Kilroy was here

Writing Frame

Name: _____ **Date:** _____

Write a news report about something happening in your town which makes you angry or upset.

<table>
<tr><td>

News Reports

- Are written in columns
- Have a headline
- Have a quote of what someone says
- Have a picture of the event.

</td><td>

Planning a Report

Remember the 4Ws

Who?   When?

Where?   What?

</td></tr>
</table>

Ideas e.g. vandalism; car crime; bullying; swearing; pollution; building works etc.

Headline: _____

Who?

When?

Where?

What ?

Quote:

Daily News
March 29th 1912

Race For The South Pole

Report by Tom Smith

Captain Robert Falcon Scott died on his way back from the South Pole.

On March 28th Scott and his fellow travellers froze to death in a snow storm.

He had been trying to return from the South Pole having been beaten by another man.

His diary told everything that had happened.

Everything was going well until the weather got worse on the way home. It was so bad they had to stay in their tents. There wasn't much fuel left to cook with or keep them warm.

Evans died on February 10th after a bad fall. On the night of 20th February Captain Oats disappeared. He was afraid he was slowing everyone down.

Robert Scott wrote in his diary, "How I wish we were home, safe and sound with our families."

His family were too upset to speak. Robert Scott will be sadly missed.

How to Write a News Report

Name: _____ **Date:** _____

Write your own news report about an exciting event in history.

News Reports

- Are written in columns
- Have a headline
- Write what someone has said
- Have a picture.

Planning a Report

Remember the 4W's

Who?   When?

Where?   What?

Ideas for a news report:

Headline: _____

Who?

When?

Where?

What ?

Include what someone said:

Word Bank

Great Fire of London

Great Plague

Battle of Hastings

Tomb of Tutankhamun

explorer e.g. Edmund Hillary

invention
car
aeroplane
television
computers
moon landing

war
September 11th 2001

How to Write a News Report

Name: _____ **Date:** _____

Write your own news report about an exciting event in history.

News Reports

- Are written in columns
- Have a headline
- Have a quote of what someone says
- Have a picture of the event.

Planning a Report

Remember the 4Ws

Who?   When?

Where?   What?

Ideas e.g. Great Fire; The Plague; Explorers; Inventions; Battles etc.

Headline: _____

Who?

When?

Where?

What ?

Quote:

Advertisements

- Are colourful

- Use big bold headings

- Use clear words

- Exaggerate.

Example 1

Smiler's Island Homes

For Sale - Paradise Island - where dreams come true!

Location   1 mile from Splash Point

Includes:
- 5 bedroomed home with fresh running water
- hundreds of miles of white sandy beaches
- forest with rare species of animals
- clear blue waters with tropical fish (no sharks!)
- helicopter pad
- motor boat (latest design)
- diving equipment

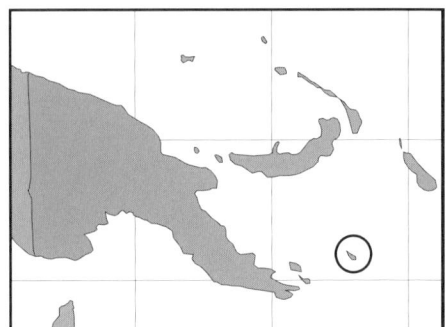

Price: Offers around £2 million.

Telephone - **0202 061 486 375**

How to Write an Advertisement

Name: _____ **Date:** _____

Write an advertisement for an island which is for sale.

Advertisements

- Are colourful
- Use big bold headings
- Use clear language
- Are short and to the point.

Planning Advertisements

- Choose bright colours for the title and headings
- Draw a colourful picture
- Choose your words carefully.

Ideas for the advertisement:

Large Title: _____

Sketch of island:

Ideas for a map:

What is for sale?

Where is it?

What do you get?

Price: _____ Telephone number: _____

Word Bank

island

house

boat

beach

fish

shells

stream

forest

rock pools

pure white

sandy

golden

sweet

smelling

fresh

clear blue

33

How to Write an Advertisement

Name:_____ **Date:** _____

Write an advertisement for an island which is for sale.

Advertisements
- Are colourful and bright
- Use big bold headings and titles
- Use clever language
- Are short and to the point.

Planning Advertisements
- Choose bright colours for the title and headings
- Draw a colourful picture
- Choose your words carefully.

Ideas: dazzling white beach; ivory coloured shells; bubbling stream etc.

Large Title: _____

Sketch of island:

Ideas for a map:

What is for sale?

Where is it?

What do you get?

Price: Telephone number:

Example 2

Wacky Inventions

Hippy Hair!

Hair for all occasions!

The ideal present for all ages. Just add the coloured paint provided to your normal shampoo. Rub onto your head. In seconds you have the hair colour of your dreams! Washes out in warm water.

For special occasions try the Glitter Goop! A hair dye which sparkles!!!

NASTY NAILS

Be a winner at fancy dress parties!

Buy nasty nails! Just like the real thing!
Spray on and leave to dry.

Your nails will double in length in just two minutes.
Enough spray to last a year.

How to Write an Advertisement

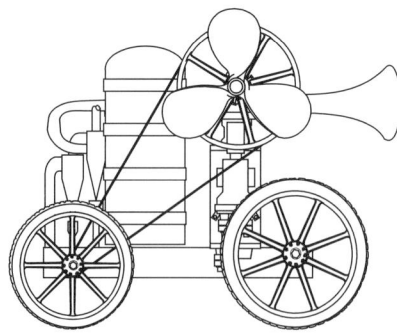

Name: _____ **Date:** _____

Design a poster advertising a strange invention.

Advertisements
- Are colourful
- Have big bold headings
- Use clear language
- Exaggerate.

Planning Advertisements
- Draw what you want to advertise
- Write an exciting title in colour
- Write down some exciting words to describe it.

Drawing:

Useful Ideas

glasses

shoes

watch

ear plugs

belt

gloves

Word Bank

What do they do?

make you:

grow

jump

invisible

lazy

strong

fly

Title ideas: _____

_____

_____

What it looks like:

What does it do?

How to Write an Advertisement

Name:_____ **Date:** _____

Design a poster advertising a strange invention.

Advertisements
- Are colourful
- Have big bold headings
- Use clever language e.g. alliteration and made up words
- Exaggerate.

Planning Advertisements
- Draw what you want to advertise
- Write an exciting title in colour
- Use clever language
- Exaggerate.

Drawing:

Title ideas: _____

_____

_____

_____

_____

What it looks like:

What does it do?

How will this invention change/ improve your life?

Points of View

- Have an introduction

- Explain what the writer believes e.g. "I think that….."

- Uses words that move the argument on e.g. firstly, finally..

- Reach a conclusion e.g. "Therefore I am…"

- Uses examples to prove a point.

School Bus

Example 1

St Mark's Primary School,
Ribbon Close,
Finlay,
Westshire
7th June 2001

School Trips

Dear Parents,

I am sorry to inform you that class trips will be cancelled this year.

Firstly, the trips cost a lot of money and because not all children pay, the school has to pay towards it. However, there is no spare money in the budget to do this at the present time.

Secondly, while the children are on a school trip they are missing their lessons. Every lesson is important and a full day can mean the difference between passing or failing an exam.

Finally, there have been several cases recently in the news of accidents happening on trips. We are very worried that children may fall or hurt themselves and then we would be responsible.

Considering all these points, we have decided that in the best interest of the children the trips will be cancelled until further notice.

Yours sincerely,

D Redhead

D Redhead
Headteacher

How to Write a Point of View

School Bus

Name: _____ **Date:** _____

Write a letter to the Headteacher disagreeing with the decision to cancel school trips this year.

Points of View
- Have an introduction
- Use words like firstly, finally
- Each point is written in a paragraph
- Have a conclusion.

Planning Your Point of View
- Think of two or more reasons for your point of view
- Write each reason in a new paragraph.

Ideas for a letter with a point of view:
My point of view is:

I believe this because:

I also believe:

Considering all these points I think:

Word Bank

firstly

secondly

finally

disagree

believe

therefore

Reasons
enjoyable

fun

visit new places

learn new things

40

How to Write a Point of View

School Bus

Name: _____ **Date:** _____

Write a letter to the Headteacher disagreeing with the decision to cancel school trips this year.

Points of View
- Have an introduction
- Use words to move the argument on e.g. firstly, finally, therefore
- Have a conclusion.

Planning Your Point of View
- Think of 3 reasons for your point of view
- Write 1 reason in each paragraph.

Ideas e.g. enjoyable; fun; visit new places; learn new things etc.

Introduction:

I believe this because:

I also believe:

I also believe:

Conclusion:

Ban Homework!

Report by Harry Croft, aged 9

I think that homework should be banned.

Firstly, I think that homework should be banned because children need time to relax. If children work all day and all night then they will have no time to do what they want. They will have no time for hobbies and things they enjoy. Then when they grow up they will not know what to do with themselves when they have free time.

Secondly I think that homework should be banned because it stops people talking. If children are spending all evening in their rooms then they will have no time for family and friends. They will spend even less time with their family and this could cause problems.

Finally, I think that homework should be banned because children work hard enough during the day and they are tired at night. Adults go to work but most of them come home at night and do not do any homework.

Finally, homework can cause stress, especially if the teacher does not give homework that is at the right level. It can cause arguments in the family and sleepless nights.

Therefore, I am of the opinion that homework should be banned.

How to Write a Point of View

Name: _____ **Date:** _____

Write a report with the point of view that homework is good for young children.

Points of View
- Have an introduction
- Use words like firstly, finally
- Each point is written in a paragraph.

Planning Points of View
- Think of two or more reasons for your point of view
- Write 1 reason in each paragraph
- Use words like firstly.

Ideas for a report with a point of view:
My point of view is:

I believe this because:

I also believe:

Considering all these points I think:

Word Bank

firstly

secondly

finally

however

therefore

Reasons

get ready for

High School

develop

concentration

learn new

things

revision

How to Write a Point of View

Name: _____ **Date:** _____

Write a report with the point of view that homework is a good thing for young children to do.

Instructions
- Have an introduction
- Use words to move the argument on e.g. firstly, finally, therefore
- Each point is written in a paragraph.

Planning Instructions
- Think of 3 reasons for your point of view
- Write 1 reason in each paragraph.

Ideas e.g. preparation for High School; develop concentration; learn new things etc.
Introduction:

I believe this because:

I also believe:

I also believe:

Conclusion:

School on Saturdays!

Talk given by Sammy Jones, Y11 at the Debating Club, of Kingswood High School.

I believe that children should go to school on Saturdays. These are my reasons.

Firstly, children are not getting enough education. They have short days during the week and teachers are finding it hard to fit in all the lessons. If children go to school on Saturday, they will learn a lot more and standards will go up!

Secondly, if children go to school on Saturdays it will give their parents some free time. Parents will be able to do the shopping without their children getting in the way and they will be able to get jobs done like housework and DIY.

Finally, teachers get far too many holidays. They get paid during the holidays, which is unfair as some other people only get paid for the work they do. If they worked Saturdays this would be much fairer.

Therefore, I am very much of the opinion that school on Saturdays would be a very good idea, and hope that other people will agree with me.

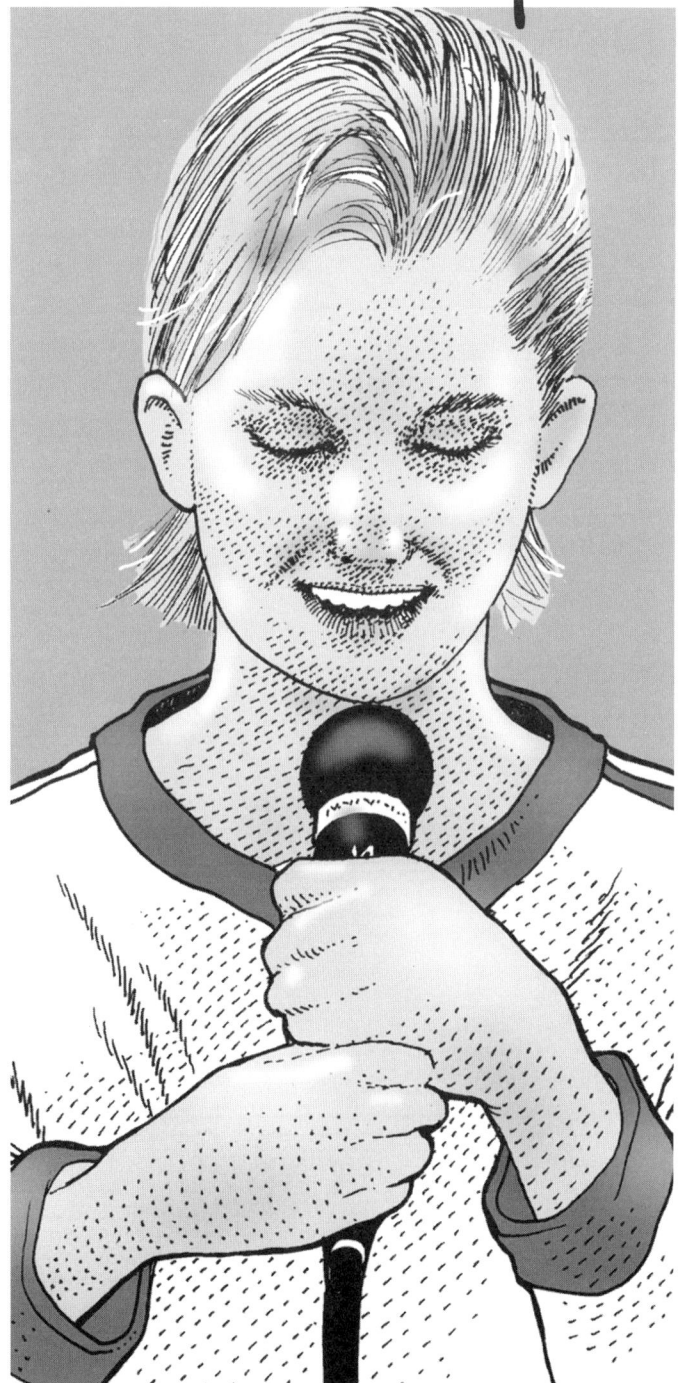

How to Write a Point of View

Name: _____ **Date:** _____

Write a speech to read to other children saying why school should not open on Saturdays.

Points of View
- Have an introduction
- Use words like firstly, finally
- Each point is written in a paragraph
- There is a conclusion.

Planning Points of View
- What do you believe?
- Think of two or more reasons why you believe it.
- Give facts and information to back up what you say

Ideas for a speech with a point of view:
My point of view is:

I believe this because:

I also believe:

Considering all these points I think:

Word Bank

believe

children

school

Saturdays

Ideas

tired

family time

teachers work too hard

electricity

staff

school dinners

How to Write a Point of View

Name:_____ **Date:** _____

Write a speech to read to other children saying why school should not open on Saturdays.

Instructions
- Have an introduction
- Use words like firstly, finally
- Each point is written in a paragraph
- There is a conclusion.

Planning Instructions
- What do you believe?
- Think of two or more reasons why you believe it
- Give facts and information to back up what you say.

Ideas e.g. all work and no play is dull; visit friends and family; sport and hobbies etc.
Introduction:

I believe this because:

I also believe:

I also believe:

Conclusion:

Shortened Forms

Diagrams
- Are drawn carefully
- Have labels
- Have arrows pointing to important parts

Key Words
- Are usually naming words
  e.g. grass
- Are arranged in groups
  e.g. Mountain sheep,
  Down sheep, Longwool sheep

Notes
- Are usually important words only
- Use naming words
  e.g. animals, leaves
- Arrange the words in order
- Arrange the words in groups.

Example 1
(Diagrams)

Helicopters

Helicopters have main rotor blades, which spin around very quickly.

They also have tail rotor blades.

A helicopter has a landing skid so that it can land gently.

The pilot controls the helicopter by using the joystick.

He also uses foot pedals.

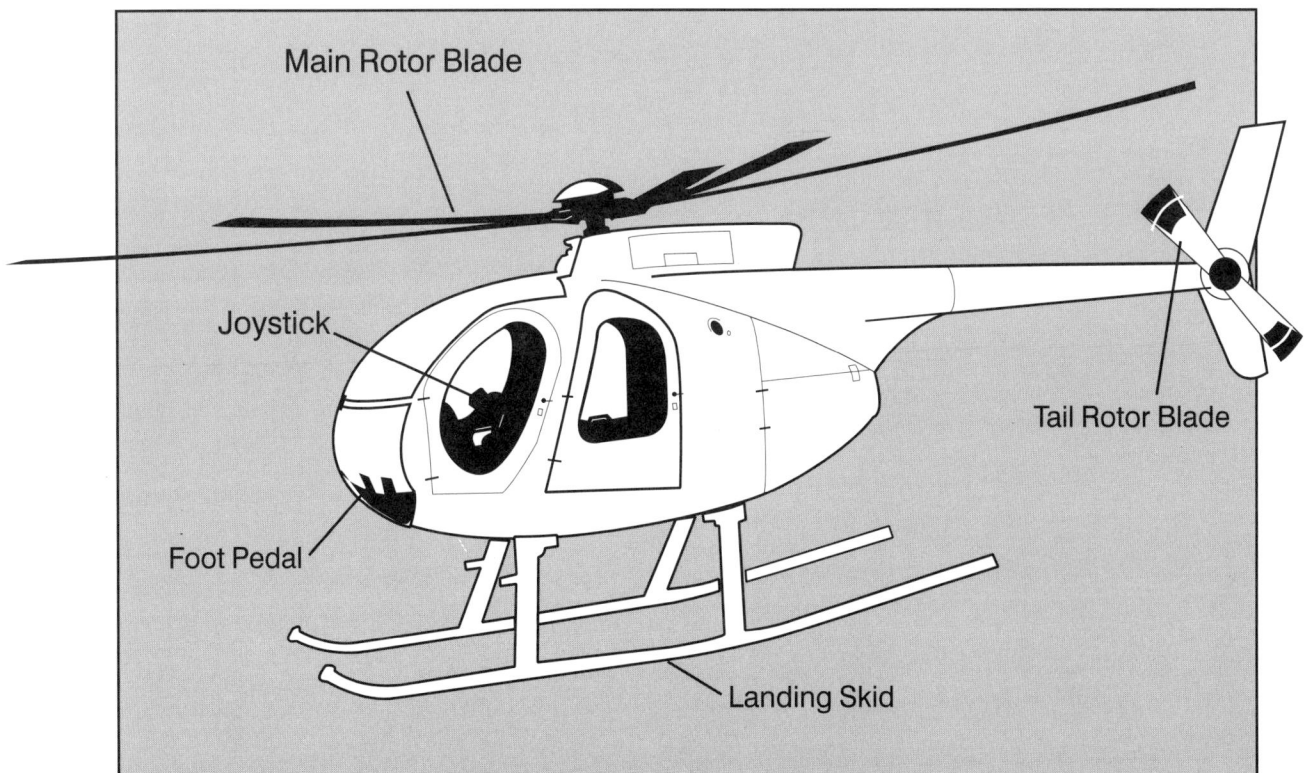

Main Rotor Blade

Joystick

Tail Rotor Blade

Foot Pedal

Landing Skid

How to Write Shortened Forms
(Diagrams)

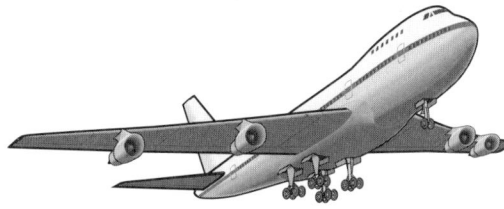

Name: _____ **Date:** _____

Draw a car. Label it carefully.

Diagrams
- Are drawn carefully
- Have labels showing the important parts
- Have arrows pointing to the parts from the labels.

Planning Your Diagram
- Find pictures of cars
- Sketch your choice of car
- Draw arrows pointing to the important parts
- Label the important parts.

Ideas for a diagram of a car:

Title _____

Sketch your car below. Write labels and draw arrows to the parts.

Word Bank

car

bonnet

wing

registration number

wipers

door handle

boot

wheel

trim

tyre

headlight

How to Write
Shortened Forms
(Diagrams)

Name:_____ **Date:** _____

Draw a form of transport. Label it carefully

Diagrams	Planning Your Diagram
• Are drawn carefully • Have labels showing the important parts • Have arrows pointing to the important parts.	• Choose a kind of transport • Draw it carefully using a ruler to help • Draw arrows with a ruler pointing to the important parts • Label the important parts.

Title: _____

Example 2
(Key Words)

Farm Animals

Sheep

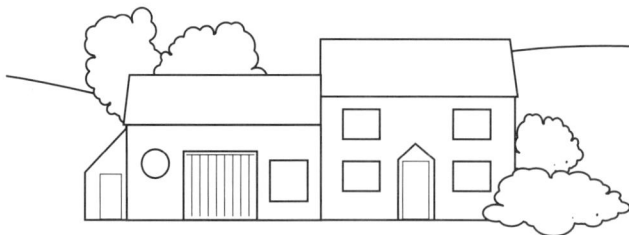

Sheep are animals. They eat grass, swedes and turnips. There are lots of different kinds of sheep.

Mountain Sheep

Mountain Sheep are smaller than most other breeds. They can live on poor grass. The meat from the mountain sheep is very good.

Down Sheep

Down Sheep live on lower ground and are fairly small. Their wool is short. Their meat is lean with little fat.

Longwool Sheep

These sheep are bigger than the others and they give more meat. Most of them have white faces.

Sheep – *Key Words*

Sheep	Mountain	Down	Longwool
animals	small	lower ground	big
grass	poor grass	small	more meat
turnips	good meat	short wool	white faces
swede		lean meat	
different kinds			

How to Write Shortened Forms
(Key Words)

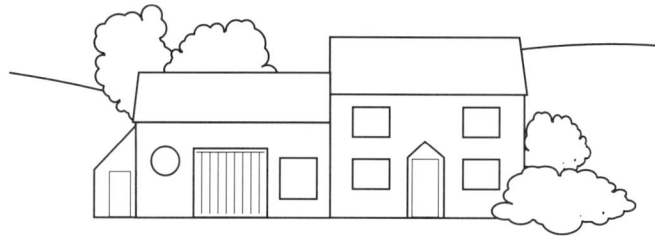

Name: _____ **Date:** _____

Read some information about a farm animal. Write down the key words

Key Words
- Usually naming words
- Written in order
- Arranged in groups.

Writing Key Words
- Read the information
- Write down the nouns
- Write the words in groups.

My ideas for key words:

Title: _____

Word Bank

cows

grass

fields

milk

cheese

beef

steak

pigs

pig sty

slops

pork bacon

gammon

chickens

corn

eggs

How to Write
Shortened Forms
(Key Words)

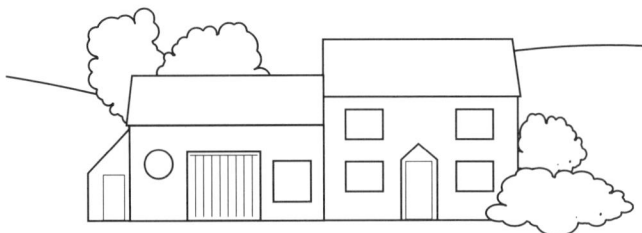

Name:_____ **Date:** _____

Read some information about a farm animal. Write down the key words.

Key Words	Writing Key Words
• Usually naming words • Written in order • Arranged in groups.	• Read the information • Write down the nouns • Write the words in groups.

Key Words

Title _____

Earthworms

Earthworms are animals. They do not have any ears. They do not have any eyes. They do not have any legs.

Earthworms live in the soil under the ground. They tunnel through the soil. They have tiny bristles which help them grip as they move along.

At night, earthworms come out of the soil to look for food like dead leaves. They pull the leaves down into their burrows where they can eat them safely. They also like to eat animal remains. The leftovers are pushed up above the ground, making small heaps called worm casts.

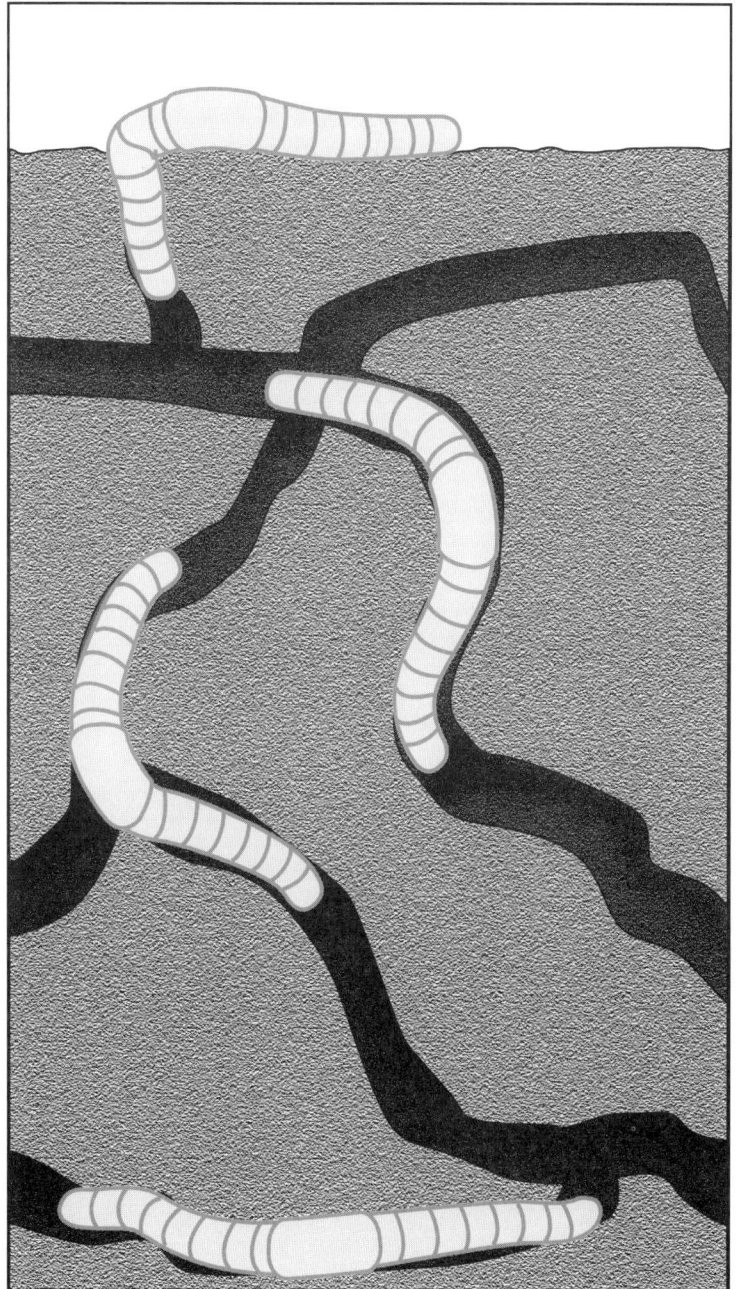

My notes on Earthworms
by Jack Heap

Earth worms — animals, no eyes, ears, legs

Live under ground, tunnel through soil, bristles help them grip

Night time — eat food, leaves, dead animals, leftovers push up, make worm casts

How to Write
Shortened Forms
(Notes)

Name: _____ **Date:** _____

Read some information about small animals or insects e.g. butterflies, ladybirds, ants etc. and then make notes about them.

Notes
- Write the most important words
- Use mainly nouns (naming words)
- Arrange the words in order
- Arrange the words in groups.

Making Notes
- Read the information first
- Write down the important words only
- Write the words in groups.

My ideas for notes:

Title _____

Word Bank

insect

animal

ladybird

beetle

ant

bee

body

head

legs

eyes

wings

antennae

fly

colour

food

home

How to Write
Shortened Forms
(Notes)

Writing
Frame

Name: _____ **Date:** _____

Read some information about insects e.g. butterflies, ladybirds, ants etc.
Make detailed notes about them.

Notes
- Write the most important words
- Use mainly nouns
- Arrange words in order
- Arrange words in groups.

Making Notes
- Read the information first
- Write down only the important words
- Write the words in groups.

Notes

Title _____

Explanations

- Are written in the present tense
  e.g. Beavers live in lodges

- Use technical words
  e.g. The moisture from the air
  may collect in special ways.

- Are impersonal
  e.g. You can see frost.

- Use diagrams

Example 1

Animal Homes
How Do Beavers Build Lodges?

Many animals and birds build homes. Some homes are very clever and will have taken a long time to build.

Beavers live in lodges. They sleep in them, hide from enemies and have babies in them.

How do Beavers build lodges?

1. First they cut down trees and carry them to a river to make a dam.
2. Next they use mud to fill up the gaps and stop the water getting through.
3. They usually build their home on top of the dam.
4. Sometimes they build their home on a small island or around a bushy tree in the middle of the river.
5. They pile up branches in the shape of a dome and cement them together with mud to make the walls.
6. The roof is not filled with mud so that the air can get inside.
7. They leave a space at the bottom to make a tunnel that goes into the river.

How to Write an Explanation

Name: _____ **Date:** _____

Look at books about birds. Choose one bird and write an explanation about how it builds its nest.

Explanations
- Written in the present tense - e.g. now
- Use words like 'they' and 'you'
- Use diagrams.

Planning Your Explanation
- Write a title
- Write an opening sentence
- Write why they build nests
- Write how they make the nest
- Use numbers.

Ideas for an explanation:

Title:

_____

_____

_____

Opening sentence:

Why:

How:

1)

2)

3)

4)

Diagram:

Word Bank

nest

tree

hedge

gutter

branches

twigs

leaves

grass

feathers

mud

stick

shape

How to Write an Explanation

Name:_____ **Date:** _____

Look at books about birds. Choose one bird and write an explanation about how it builds its nest.

Instructions
- Written in the present tense – e.g. now
- Use words like 'they' and 'you'
- Use diagrams.

Planning Instructions
- Write a title
- Write an opening sentence
- Write why they make the nest
- Write how they make the nest
- Use numbers.

Ideas for an explanation:

Title:

_____

_____

Diagram:

Opening sentence:

Why:

How:

1)

2)

3)

4)

5)

Weather

Why does frost on the window look like ferns?

If the weather is very cold you can see frost on windows.

What is frost?

Frost is made of tiny bits of ice. The ice comes from moisture floating in the air.

What happens when the moisture meets the cold glass?

When the moisture meets the cold glass it makes ice crystals. The crystals make leafy shapes like ice ferns.

Do the shapes change when the temperature changes?

When it is just below freezing the crystals are flat, six sided shapes. If it is colder, the crystals are shaped like needles. If it is very cold, leafy shapes appear.

Why does this happen?

a. The ice patterns sometimes start to grow along fine scratches in the glass.

b. The moisture from the air may collect around specks of dust along the window sill.

c. The moisture may collect on a film of soap left from washing windows.

How to Write an Explanation

Writing Support Sheet

Name: _____ **Date:** _____

Explain why it sometimes snows in winter.

Explanations
- Answer a question or explain something
- Are written in the present tense
- May use diagrams.

Planning Your Explanation
- Find the information you need
- Write the title and opening sentence
- Use numbers to list what happens
- Draw a diagram.

Ideas for an explanation:

Title:

_____

_____

_____

Opening sentence:

Diagram:

Word Bank

water cycle

water vapour

drops of water

clouds

sky

heavy

rain

below freezing

snow

What happens:

1)

2)

3)

4)

5)

How to Write an Explanation

Writing Frame

Name:_____ **Date:** _____

Explain why it sometimes snows in winter.

Explanations
- Answer a question or explain something
- Written in the present tense
- May use diagrams.

Planning Your Explanation
- Research the information
- Write the title and introduction
- Use numbers to list what happens
- Draw a diagram and label it.

Ideas for an explanation:

Title:

_____

_____

Diagram:

Introduction:

How it snows:

1)

2)

3)

4)

5)

6)

7)

8)